Top Ten Reasons Your Novel is Rejected

and How to Avoid Them

LOIS WINSTON

Cover design by L. Winston

ISBN-13: 978-1-940795-22-5

DEDICATION

To my husband Rob for encouraging me to follow my muse

CONTENTS

ACKNOWLEDGMENTS

Special thanks to all the authors who came before me from whom I've learned so much and the publishing professionals who continue to educate me.

No matter how diligent we are nor how many times we proof our own work, another set of eyes always catches something we miss. Special thanks to author Irene Peterson for her editing expertise and being my extra set of eyes on this book.

I'd also like to thank all the writers who have taken my workshops over the years and who urged me to make the information contained in this book available to others.

.

INTRODUCTION

Over the years, I've given workshops and talks to several thousand aspiring writers. As an agent, I've listened to hundreds of pitches and read through tens of thousands of query letters and manuscript submissions. Being both a published author and a literary agent has given me a unique perspective. I know what it's like to be the writer whose only desire is to sell a novel, and I know what it's like to have to crush someone's hopes with a rejection letter. It wasn't until I started sending out those rejection letters that I began to have a better understanding of why so many writers receive them.

What I've come to realize is that most manuscripts are rejected by agents and editors for one or more of ten basic reasons. Writers have control over some of these reasons but not all of them. This book will discuss these ten reasons and how you can control more of your destiny by not falling prey to them. This is not a list where I save the best (or worst) for last. There's no ascending or descending order to the list because not every item on the list will apply to every writer. For some of you, only one item will pertain. For others, some or many.

1

YOU HAVEN'T DONE YOUR HOMEWORK

This really shouldn't even be a reason, but it's one of the top reasons most writers are rejected by editors and agents. You'd think that if someone spent months or even years writing a book, that person would at least devote a few hours into researching editors and agents. Sadly, most don't. I can't tell you how many queries I read that are for types of books our agency doesn't handle. Other agents will tell you the same thing. Editors have a similar lament.

Do your research. There are many places on the Internet, as well as books available that will give you basic information about what editors and agents want. All publishers and many agencies have websites. Many editors and agents have blogs. And even if an agent has neither a blog nor a website, the agency most likely has a listing on Publishers Marketplace and will be listed in the various yearly guides that are published. Check these sites and publications for current information regarding books agents have recently sold and editors have recently bought. You'll also learn what they're looking for and what they no longer want to see in the way of submissions. Editors and agents don't want to be bombarded with queries for books they don't publish or handle. It's a waste of time for both you and them.

Do You Know What You Write?

Even before you make a list of the agents and editors who handle what you write, you first need to know what you write. Seems pretty basic, doesn't it? Apparently not. It's amazing how many writers are totally clueless about genre. Take this exchange, for example, between an agent and a writer during a speed pitching session at a recent conference:

Agent: So tell me about your book.

Writer: It's a mystery called *The Whodunit Caper*.

Agent: What kind of mystery?

Writer: The kind where there's a murder and my heroine, a middle-aged former go-go dancer who now works as a customer service rep for a car dealership, figures out who did it.

Agent: So this is a cozy mystery?

Writer: Well, she does get cozy with the parts salesman, but she's also got an ex who wants to get back together, and she's torn between them. And she's also developing the hots for the detective on the case, so there's lots of sex when she's not trying to figure out who the killer is. So I guess it's a three-way cozy.

—

I'm sure many of you are rolling your eyes over our clueless writer. Unfortunately, there are too many of them out there.

Popular commercial fiction is divided into genres. Romance, mystery, and speculative fiction are the three biggies. However, each of these genres is also divided up into sub-genres, and sometimes the sub-genres are divided even further. For instance, romance is broken down into category romance and single title romance, but these two categories are broken up even further to include contemporary romance, historical romance, young adult romance, erotic romance, inspirational romance, paranormal romance, and romantic suspense. Speculative fiction will encompass science fiction, urban fantasy, epic fantasies, horror, time travel, alternative history, dystopian and utopian fiction, space operas, and supernatural fiction. Mystery will include cozy mysteries, amateur sleuth mysteries, soft-boiled mysteries, hard-boiled mysteries, detective mysteries, noir mysteries, police procedurals, thrillers, suspense, and historical mysteries.

Some of these genres and sub-genres have specific word counts that must be adhered to; others need to keep to certain conventions. As a writer you not only need to know which genre your work falls into but which sub-genre or sub-sub-genre because there are different conventions for each. A cozy mystery won't have graphic violence or sex. An editor who buys only hard-boiled detective novels is not going to be interested in amateur sleuth books. An agent who handles romance may only want single title romance and not be interested in seeing either category romance or inspirational romance.

Most of these categories can also be found within middle grade and young adult fiction. And just to complicate matters further, more and more books are now combining genres. For instance, you can have a romantic mystery or a middle grade time travel mystery, or an alternate history romantic mystery. What you can't have is a middle grade erotic time travel mystery. Or a middle grade erotic anything, for that matter. So learn what the genres and sub-genres are and what you can and can't do within each.

Some Genre and Sub-genre Definitions

Romance: Whether a romance is a category romance or a single title romance, the one rule to remember is that **all romances must have a happily-ever-after ending**. If the book ends with a satisfying ending but not a happily-ever-after, it's not considered romance. Romances are broken up into category and single title romances, then broken up further into contemporary, historical, inspirational (either contemporary or historical) and speculative (generally, paranormal, fantasy, and futuristic.) Romantic suspense can fall within any of these sub-genres as well.

Category (or Series) Romance: These books are published primarily by Harlequin. They're released each month and remain on store shelves for only one month. Then they're pulled to make way for the next month's releases. Word counts range from 50,000–75,000 words, depending on the line. (A manuscript less than 50,000 words is generally considered a novella.) Category romances focus on the relationship between the hero and heroine. Plot plays a secondary role to the relationship. There are generally only two points of view in these books, the hero's and the heroine's, and because of the shorter length, there are rarely any sub-plots and few secondary characters, although you will find some sub-plots and more secondary characters in longer lines.

Single Title Romance: These are the books that remain on store shelves for as long as they're selling (Sort of. Unless you're a bestselling author with a backlist, your book will be pulled within 3-6 months of release to make way for newer releases.) While concentrating on the relationship between the hero and heroine, the plots are more involved. They usually contain secondary characters and at least one subplot, often more. Length is generally 80,000–110,000 words. As with category romances, the love story between the hero and heroine is always the main focus of the single title romance.

Romantic Suspense: These are books where the suspense is a major element of the plot. The suspense plot is blended with the love story, and there's always a happily-ever-after ending. The balance of suspense to romance will vary. For the category romantic suspense lines, the balance is generally 65-70% romance/30-35% suspense. For single title, the ratio can be as much as 50% romance/50% suspense. If the romance is less than 50% of the book, it's not a romantic suspense; it's straight suspense with a romantic element of some degree.

Inspirational Fiction: These are novels in which an inspirational message of personal religious faith is a major element of the story. They can be either romances or not, contemporary or historical. If the story contains a romance, the level of sensuality is extremely low with absolutely no sex scenes. There is also no foul language or graphic violence.

Women's Fiction: Women's fiction is more a marketing concept than a genre. What it means is that the book is a type of general fiction that will appeal predominantly to women. Strange, considering there's no similar marketing concept called "men's fiction" for books that appeal predominantly to men. But since the term is used by many, I thought it important to tell you what it is and what it isn't.

Women's Fiction is *not* romance, although it can contain a romance, sometimes as a strong secondary plot, sometimes as a minor element to the story. There may not be a hero in women's fiction. The love story, if there is one, is not the main focus of women's fiction, and there doesn't have to be a happily-ever-after ending. However, there should be an emotionally satisfying ending. Women's fiction is a sub-genre of mainstream novels (books that are more plot-driven than literary fiction but contain less of the mandatory conventions of genre fiction.) These books are shelved under general fiction in bookstores. Word count is generally 80,000–125,000 words and can be broken down into sub-genres that include chick lit, hen lit, mommy lit, relationship stories, sagas, coming-of-age novels, and more.

Erotica: Webster's defines *erotica* as "erotic books or pictures" and *erotic* as "of or arousing sexual feelings or desires; having to do with sexual love." Erotica are books that contain a high level of sexual content. They are sexually explicit stories, daring stories with graphic details that often push the envelope. Erotica can be contemporary, historical, or any one of the genres within the romance fiction umbrella.

Young Adult Fiction: Young adult (or YA novels) are books geared toward junior and senior high school students. The plots primarily revolve around the relationships and lives of characters within that age group and can be contemporary, historical, mysteries, or speculative fiction. The level of sensuality is usually tame, although some publishers have been known to push the envelope.

New Adult Ficiton: Books are similar to Young Adult fiction, but the protagonists are older, generally 18-25, and for the first time confronting issues as legal adults. Sex scenes are permissible.

Mysteries: These are stories in which one or more element remains unknown or unexplained until the end of the story. In the mystery, a crime (often murder) has been or will be committed, and the protagonist's goal is to solve the crime. Mysteries deal with the "who" of a story (hence, the "whodunit.")

Cozy or Traditional Mysteries: Stories where the crime and all violence occur "off-stage." These books also contain no foul language or explicit sex.

Amateur Sleuth Mysteries: Stories where the crime solver doesn't work in law enforcement.

Soft-boiled Mysteries: Stories that contain some violence and profanity but are not as graphic as hardboiled mysteries. The protagonist is often a female detective.

Hardboiled Mysteries: Darker stories that contain violence, graphic description, and/or profanity. The protagonist is generally a detective.

Police Procedurals: Stories that involve the investigation of a crime by the police.

Suspense: These stories fall under the general mystery umbrella, but they deal more with the psychology behind why the antagonist committed the crime, why he chose his victims, and why the protagonist cares enough to get involved in helping bring down the antagonist. The crime generally impacts a small group of people such as a family, business, or town and often involves murder or kidnapping. Sometimes in a suspense, the reader knows "whodunit" because the antagonist is a point of view character.

Thrillers: Like suspense, these stories also fall under the mystery umbrella but are more action/adventure in nature. They focus on the "how" of the story and concern larger problems that will impact a great number of people, perhaps an entire city, country, or the world. The plot focuses on the protagonist(s) trying to prevent something terrible from happening. Often, they must overcome overwhelming odds that can be either internally or externally motivated or both.

Graphic Novels: Stories, either original or adapted, that are written in comic book format or as heavily illustrated paperbacks.

Speculative Fiction: This is the all-inclusive term for science fiction, horror, fantasy, etc.

Horror: Disturbing stories, either entirely psychological in nature or involving the supernatural, that are meant to terrify or horrify the reader by creating an atmosphere of fear or dread.

Science Fiction: Stories that must incorporate an element of science in either the plot or setting. Stories often, but not always, take place in the future or on another planet or in another galaxy.

Fantasy: Stories that incorporate magic and/or mythology in the characters, plot, and/or setting.

Urban Fantasy: Stories that place magical characters in contemporary settings, generally in the present day or the future.

Westerns: This is the only genre totally defined by location and time period. Stories generally involve a rugged hero facing down adversity of some sort in the 1800s west of the Missouri River. Many will incorporate a strong romance, but romance isn't a pre-requisite of a western.

Historical Fiction: Stories set in the past where the plot will revolve around actual historical events and/or people of the period. Sometimes the protagonist is an historical figure, but part or all of the story is fictitious.

Other times the protagonist is a fictional person placed into real events of the time.

Literary Fiction: These books are all about the genius of the author as a wordsmith. The plot can be minimal, and often the protagonist doesn't experience any character growth.

Mainstream Fiction: Non-genre specific fiction other than literary fiction that appeals to a general readership. The books are generally set in present day and involve universal themes that appeal to a broad demographic.

Finally, keep in mind what I stated earlier. Lines are blurring in popular fiction. So it's often hard to pigeon-hole a book when pitching it to an editor or agent. How do you categorize your book? Sometimes that's the million-dollar question. Having a good understanding of the various genres should help you. And hey, when all else fails, make up a new genre. You could turn out to be on the cutting edge of a new trend.

Ways to Research What Agents Handle and What Editors Buy

Not only should you research editors and agents by the genres they handle, but by the individual books they've recently bought and sold. An agent who handles suspense might only like gritty suspense, not romantic suspense. An editor who buys YA (young adult) books might only want historicals and contemporaries, not paranormals, and not because she doesn't like paranormals but because she already has enough and needs to balance out her list.

So do your homework and save yourself the sting of receiving a lot of form rejection letters. Here are some sources to get you stared:

Publishers Marketplace
www.publishersmarketplace.com
This site has both a paid version and an abbreviated free version. Editors and agents often post sales on the site. Many agents have a page that lists what they

handle and how to submit. One caveat, though: some agents don't believe in posting their sales. They feel that this information is proprietary between the author, the agent, and the publisher. So just because you don't see a listing of sales for the agent or agency, it doesn't mean there haven't been sales.

Association of Authors' Representatives
www.aaronline.org

AAR is an organization of independent literary and dramatic agents. All AAR members must adhere to a strict code of ethics which includes not charging fees for reading manuscripts. There are a lot of scams that prey on needy writers. Make sure the agencies you query are members of AAR. Not every agent in the agency needs to be a member of AAR, but the head agents should be members. AAR also has a database where you can search for agents.

Agent Query
www.agentquery.com

This site contains a large database of literary agents.

Predators and Editors
www.pred-ed.com

This site not only has a database of both agents and publishers but a rating criteria for them.

Jeff Herman's Guide to Book Publishers, Editors, and Literary Agents
http://www.jeffherman.com/store/jeff-hermans-guide-to-book-publishers-editors-and-literary-agents/

Jeff Herman is both an agent and the author of this extensive yearly guide.

In addition, there are writing organizations with many resources for their members. Some have websites with resources for non-members as well as members. These include:

American Crime Writers League
www.acwl.org

Authors Guild
www.authorsguild.org

Horror Writers Association
www.horror.org

International Thriller Writers
www.thrillerwriters.org

Liberty States Fiction Writers
www.lsfwriters.com

Mystery Writers of America
www.mysterywriters.org

Novelists Inc.
www.ninc.com

Romance Writers of America
www.rwa.org

Science Fiction and Fantasy Writers
www.sfwa.org

Sisters in Crime
www.sistersincrime.org

Western Writers of America
www.westernwriters.org

Also, Google individual publishers, editors, and agents to find their websites and blogs. Once you're armed with the proper information, you won't receive a rejection letter due to cluelessness.

2

SLOPPY EDITING AND/OR PROOFING

You sabotage yourself by failing to proofread your work and by not having a good command of the English language.

No manuscript was ever rejected because of a few typos, but if you've got typos on the first page of your manuscript, I probably won't read the second page, and neither will many other agents or editors. If you can't take the time to make sure your work is being sent out in as perfect a shape as possible, why should I take the time to read it? And trust me, I'm not unique in feeling this way.

When it comes to grammar, though, writers have the license to take liberties. When you're writing dialogue, no one expects it to be written in perfectly formed sentences. People don't always speak in perfectly formed sentences; we speak in sentence fragments. Style often dictates that sentence fragments also be used in narrative.

However, there are grammar rules that should never be broken. If your head is buzzing with story ideas, but English class is a distant, buried memory and spelling was never your strong suit, do yourself a couple of favors. First, learn how to master the Spell Check function on your computer, but don't set it to correct automatically. After all, it's a computer and sometimes thinks you mean one word when you mean another.

Next, buy a good grammar and punctuation book. Read it from cover to cover, and commit the rules to memory. Here are a few I recommend because they're extremely easy to understand:

• *ReWrite Right!* By Jan Venolia

• *Woe is I* by Patricia T. O'Conner

• *Self-Editing for Fiction Writers* by Renni Browne and Dave King

One thing I don't recommend is using the Grammar Check function of your word processing software. Grammar Check is great if you're writing a business letter or report. It's lousy for fiction. Disable it.

Below I've highlighted the most common grammar and punctuation errors I consistently come across. This doesn't mean they're the only errors writers make, just the ones I see made most often. Don't think by learning these few rules below that you can avoid studying those books I suggested above.

The Two Most Common Grammar Error Seen in Submissions

1. Improper Use of Pronouns

In my opinion, pronouns are the most misused words in the English language. There are three types of pronouns—the nominative, the possessive, and the objective.

Nominative: I, you, he, she, it, we, they, and who
Possessive: my, your, yours, his, her, hers, its, our, ours, their, theirs, and whose
Objective: me, you, him, her, it, us, them, and whom

Too often people use the nominative instead of the objective because they think it makes them sound more educated to use *I, he,* or *she* instead of *me, him*, or *her*. However, substituting the nominative for the objective when the objective is called for will produce the opposite result. Here are a few rules to remember when it comes to pronouns:

A. Use the objective form when the pronoun is the direct object of a sentence or is part of a prepositional phrase.

Wrong: I was getting the distinct impression that Batswin's latest theory involved Erica and I in cahoots to bump off Marlys.

Right: I was getting the distinct impression that Batswin's latest theory involved Erica and me in cahoots to bump off Marlys. (from *Assault with a Deadly Glue Gun* by Lois Winston)

Wrong: "Who else has a key besides you and I?"

Right: "Who else has a key besides you and me?" (from *Death by Killer Mop Doll* by Lois Winston)

B. If a pronoun follows **than** or **as**, mentally insert the missing words to determine the correct case.

Wrong: Alex is as tall as me.

Right: Alex is as tall as I (am.)

Wrong: My mother loves my brother more than I.

Right: My mother loves my brother more than (she loves) me.

C. Reflexive pronouns, those pronouns ending in **self** or **selves**, are used only when they refer back to the subject.

Wrong: After settling into seats at a corner table, we placed our beverage orders, a Bloody Mary for Gabe and Mimosas for Reese and myself.

Right: After settling into seats at a corner table, we placed our beverage orders, a Bloody Mary for Gabe and Mimosas for Reese and me. (from *Talk Gertie to Me* by Lois Winston)

2. Misplaced and Dangling Modifiers

A. Modifiers should be placed close to the word they modify to avoid ambiguous or unintentional meanings. One of the most famous misplaced modifiers of all time is from Groucho Marx as Captain Geoffrey T. Spalding in *Animal Crackers*:

"One morning I shot an elephant in my pajamas."

He goes on to point out his own misplaced modifier with the punch line, *"How he got in my pajamas, I don't know."*

B. A dangling modifier usually begins a sentence that has omitted what it modifies.

Wrong: "Figures," I muttered. Searching the room for another seat and finding not an empty table in the place, the normally quiet café was filled with chattering strangers who nearly drowned out the Wynton Marsalis piece playing in the background. (The café wasn't searching for a seat; the point of view character was searching for one.)

Right: "Figures," I muttered, searching the room for another seat and finding not an empty table in the place. The normally quiet café was filled with chattering strangers who nearly drowned out the Wynton Marsalis piece playing in the background. (from *Talk Gertie to Me*, by Lois Winston)

The Most Common Punctuation Errors Seen in Submissions:

Misuse of Commas and Semi-Colons

The most common punctuation errors are the misuse of the comma and semi-colon, especially in regard to compound sentences and clauses. Too many writers use one when they should be using the other.

1. Commas

Commas are used to separate independent clauses in compound sentences. An independent clause is one in which there is both a subject and verb that completes a thought. A compound sentence is a sentence where two or more independent clauses are joined by a conjunction (a connecting word): **and, or, but, for, nor, yet, so.** The comma **always** precedes the conjunction.

Wrong: I knew I wasn't operating on all cylinders this morning but I was awake enough to realize this conversation was going around in a big non-productive circle.

Right: I knew I wasn't operating on all cylinders this morning, but I was awake enough to realize this conversation was going around in a big non-productive circle. (from *Death by Killer Mop Doll* by Lois Winston)

In the example above **but** is joining two independent clauses. Both contain a subject and a verb, so a comma is required before the conjunction.

Wrong: I knew I wasn't operating on all cylinders this morning, but was awake enough to realize this conversation was going around in a big non-productive circle.

Right: I knew I wasn't operating on all cylinders this morning but was awake enough to realize this conversation was going around in a big non-productive circle.

In the example above **but** is joining one independent clause and one dependent (or subordinate) clause. A dependent clause is one that doesn't complete a thought. In this case, the second part of the sentence doesn't contain a subject, so a comma is not used before the conjunction.

Commas are also used to set off subordinate clauses at the beginning of a sentence but not at the end of a sentence.

Wrong: If Lyndella and some of the other residents agreed to an interview I didn't see where Shirley Hallstead had any veto power.

Right: If Lyndella and some of the other residents agreed to an interview, I didn't see where Shirley Hallstead had any veto power. (from *Revenge of the Crafty Corpse* by Lois Winston)

Wrong: I didn't see where Shirley Hallstead had any veto power, if Lyndella and some of the other residents agreed to an interview.

Right: I didn't see where Shirley Hallstead had any veto power if Lyndella and some of the other residents agreed to an interview. (from *Revenge of the Crafty Corpse* by Lois Winston)

2. Semi-colons
These are the most misused of all punctuation marks. There are only two uses for semi-colons.

A. Use a semi-colon to separate items in a series that contain commas.

Example: The next two days included classes in painting and drawing; pottery; sculpture; needlework, quilting, and sewing; scrap crafts; decoupage; beadwork and jewelry; and paper crafts and scrapbooking. (from *Revenge of the Crafty Corpse* by Lois Winston)

B. Use a semi-colon to join independent clauses in place of a conjunction.

Example: Her jaw dropped; her eyes grew wide. (from *Revenge of the Crafty Corpse* by Lois Winston)

C. Semi-colons should never be used to separate an independent clause and a dependent clause.

Wrong: I walked slowly to keep pace with her; even though Mephisto strained at the leash.

Right: I walked slowly to keep pace with her even though Mephisto

strained at the leash. (from *Revenge of the Crafty Corpse* by Lois Winston)

Wrong: Even though he used digital cameras for most of his photography; Zack still shot with film for certain projects and did his own developing and printing.

Right: Even though he used digital cameras for most of his photography, Zack still shot with film for certain projects and did his own developing and printing. (from *Revenge of the Crafty Corpse* by Lois Winston)

I've had writers ask me why it's so important to learn grammar and punctuation. Won't the editor correct whatever needs correcting? No, she won't. She'll simply reject the manuscript if there are too many problems with it. No editor is interested in a high maintenance author. Editors don't have the luxury of time to mollycoddle a writer who refuses to learn how to write well, no matter how good a storyteller that writer is. There are plenty of other well-written manuscripts sitting in piles on editors' desks or queued up in their IN boxes.

Even writers who have a good understanding of grammar and punctuation, often make sloppy mistakes and don't realize it. Your fingers type something; your eyes see it one way, and your brain sees it another way. Here are a couple of suggestions for minimizing dumb mistakes.

1. When you've finished your manuscript, put it aside for at least a week. Then sit down and read it with a fresh pair of eyes.

2. Print out your manuscript to proofread it. Reading your writing on the printed page will often make you see things differently from what you see on the screen.

3. Read your manuscript out loud. Your ear will not only catch errors but show you areas where the writing needs tweaking due to awkward sentence structure, run-on sentences, or poor word choices.
4. Ask a fellow writer to proof your manuscript for errors and typos. (Spell

Check isn't going to pick up that place where you typed *your* and meant *you're*.)

The same suggestions apply to query letters, cover letters once you receive a request, and your synopsis. Make sure each is as error free as possible. Remember, one error isn't going to sink your chances, but many errors will. Don't be your own worst enemy. Make sure your writing is free of errors before you send it out.

3

THE DOG IS TELLING, NOT SHOWING

Once upon a time, I was your typical desperate-to-sell-any-way-possible writer. As such, I entered many writing contests sponsored by various chapters of a national writing organization. In hindsight, I wasted a heap of money. Yes, I wound up finaling in many of those contests and even winning quite a few. However, I also wound up with many low scores and off-the-wall comments from judges who often had far less knowledge and skill than I did. These well-intentioned but misinformed writers should never have been judging in the first place, but that's a topic for another book.

Think about the game of Whisper Down the Lane, and you'll get an idea of how misinformation can be perpetuated by well-meaning but clueless writers, especially when it comes to skills that many writers have a hard time grasping. Hopefully, as you read on, you'll go from clueless on some of these subjects to having a firm understanding of them.

Point of View

I once had a contest judge write on an entry, "I don't really get Point of View, but I took off points for your use of it because I don't think you understand it, either." There was nothing wrong with the point of view in my entry.

A friend of mine once had a contest judge tell her that she'd gone into the dog's Point of View. She hadn't.

Point of View (also known as Viewpoint or POV) is often a very hard concept for a beginning writer to master. And if you don't know what it is, you don't know if you're handling it correctly.

Simply stated, Point of View is the character chosen to be the camera lens for your story, the person from whose eyes the reader sees the action unfolding. It's the telling of the story from one person's perspective.

Viewpoint is usually either first person or third person.

First person books are told by a single protagonist. They're the "I" stories and can be written either in present tense or past tense. First person POV is often used in chick lit, young adult books, and many mystery sub-genres. It can also be found in various other genres, mainstream fiction, and literary fiction. Some authors use first person narrative in romance but not to a great extent because it usually limits the author to the thoughts of only one character.

Note, I said *usually*. More on that in a bit.

First person is most often used in past tense, but it can be and is used in present tense, most often (but not exclusively) in chick lit, young adult, and literary fiction.

Example of first person present tense POV:

I sit by the window and stare out at the crowd in the street.

Example of first person past tense POV:

I sat by the window and stared out at the crowd in the street.

Third person POV is the "he/she" stories and are usually written in past tense. They can be written entirely in the viewpoint of one character or in multiple viewpoints. Third person POV is the most popular point of view used in fiction. Third person POV is almost exclusively used in past tense, although there have probably been some literary novels written in Third Person Present Tense. Off hand, I can think of only one area where Third Person Present Tense is used exclusively and that's for stage direction in plays and screenplays.

Example of third person past tense POV:

Emma sat by the window and stared out at the crowd in the street.

Example of third person present Tense POV:

Emma sits by the window and stares out at the crowd in the street.

Omniscient viewpoint, often referred to as God's point of view, is a story told through the eyes of a disembodied narrator who is privy to the thoughts of all the characters. Omniscient POV is considered archaic and is generally not used in today's commercial fiction (any genre) because it distances the reader from the story. However, you can still find it in some literary novels.

Once upon a time nearly all romances were told strictly through the eyes or point of view of the heroine. Most romance novels today will employ at least two points of view, generally the hero's and heroine's. Many books will also include the POV of one or some secondary characters. Multiple points of view allow an author to tell a bigger story because he/she can enter the thoughts of more than one or two characters.

However, if a book is written in multiple points of view, the writer needs to know how to handle point of view switches. Point of view is the viewpoint character for the scene, the person the author has chosen to convey to the reader the action and emotion of that scene. It's telling the story through the chosen character's eyes.

A crucial decision the writer must make in each scene is to choose the point of view character for that scene. The scene will have the most impact if the POV character is the one who has the most to lose at that moment. This makes for greater emotional impact. It's also the reason that omniscient POV or choosing a disinterested bystander as a POV character has come to be associated with archaic writing styles. Choosing wisely for a point of view character is as important as handling point of view shifts well.

Keep in mind that there is no rule that states each chapter must be in one character's point of view or that even each scene must only be in one character's point of view. Some authors switch POV within a scene. There are no rules that say you can't. But the author should not be moving back and forth between characters throughout the scene so that the reader feels as though she's at a ping pong match. If there is a need for a POV shift, it should be logical and smooth.

If an editor or agent needs to go back and reread a paragraph or a page because the POV shift confuses him/her, the writer hasn't handled the shift well. And if the editor or agent isn't sure whose head she's in as she's reading, the writer has failed to handle POV well. Point of view that ping pongs all over the place will give an editor or agent a reason to toss a manuscript aside.

And here's something else to keep in mind: While the author is in a particular character's point of view, she can't be telling the reader what another character is seeing, thinking, feeling, hearing, etc. For instance, if the heroine is in the living room, she can't be thinking about what the hero is seeing as he looks out his bedroom window one flight up. She has no way of even knowing that he's standing at the window. If she can't see him, she can't know what he's doing.

Also, when you're in a character's point of view, she's not going to be thinking about the color of her own hair. The hero might notice the heroine brushing a wisp of her curly auburn locks off her forehead, but she's just going to push the hair back off her face. The point of view character should never describe herself. This becomes author intrusion, the author manipulating the character's thoughts as a way to let the reader know the character's hair color, eye color, height, weight, or type of earrings she's wearing. Don't do it!

If a book is written in first person, there probably won't be any POV shifts, but there's no rule that says there can't be. I wrote *Talk Gertie to Me*, a humorous novel about a mother and her adult daughter, in first person from the point of view of the two main characters. The first person POV shifted from the mother to her daughter in alternating chapters. There are also books that are written in both first and third person. In *Finding Hope*, a romance written under my Emma Carlyle pen name, I wrote the heroine in first person and the hero in third person.

The takeaway here is that editors and agents are interested in well-written books. It doesn't matter whether you write in first person or third person, past tense or present tense. Anything works if done well. But if you don't have a firm grasp of point of view and how to use it, you'll garner a swift rejection.

Passive vs. Active Writing

Often a writer will receive a rejection letter stating that his or her writing is passive. Passive writing is when you tell your story rather than show it through active narrative, dialogue, and deep point of view. You may even have heard the phrase, "Show, don't tell." But what does that mean, and how do you do it?

When you **tell** your story, you're not involving the reader, letting him or her experience the events and emotions of the story along with the characters. **Showing** engages the reader in the story and makes the reader one with the characters.

Here's an example: Picture yourself at Christmas time with your nose pressed to the glass of one of Macy's holiday display windows. That's **telling**. Now imagine yourself transported inside and becoming one of the figures in the diorama. That's **showing**. In other words, **telling** leaves the reader on the outside looking in; **showing** pulls the reader through the window and sticks him or her right in the middle of the scene, seeing and feeling all that the character is seeing and feeling.

There are several ways to show your story instead of telling it.

1. Use Dialogue

Instead of telling the reader that the character feels a certain way, show how the character feels by incorporating the emotion into a dialogue scene.

Example of Telling Through Lack of Dialogue:

As Emma and Logan sat drinking their coffee, they were interrupted by the young nanny of one of Emma's neighbors. She was pushing a stroller with a baby and dragging along a toddler. The nanny, Jana-Lynne, started gushing over Logan. She'd never met a celebrity before. She pulled a notebook and pen from her knapsack and asked Logan for his autograph, spelling out her name to make sure he got it right. Emma raised an eyebrow when Jana-Lynne asked Logan to make the autograph out to his *good friend* Jana-Lynne.

Suddenly the toddler began to have a tantrum, waking the baby, who began to howl. Logan scrawled his name and slipped the notebook back into the knapsack. Then he whispered to Emma, asking her if she'd like to make a run for it.

Example of Showing Through Use of Dialogue:

"Why, you're Logan Crawford, aren't you?" A woman in her early twenties, pushing a baby stroller and dragging a toddler in tow, parked herself in front of their table. She nodded toward Emma. "Hey, Emma, you know Logan Crawford? Cool! You don't mind if we join you, right? I've never met a real live celebrity before."

She whipped out a notebook and pen from her knapsack and thrust them at Logan. "I have got to have an autograph. No one is going to believe I met Logan Crawford unless I have proof, you know?" She jabbed at the paper. "Make it out to 'my good friend Jana-Lynne,' okay? Capital J, A, N, A, hyphen, Capital L, Y, double-N, E. Got it?"

Emma raised her eyebrows. "Good friend?"

Jana-Lynne giggled. "Who's going to know as long as you don't tell?"

The toddler at Jana-Lynne's side stamped her foot. "I wants hot chocolate."

"In a minute, sugar. I'm busy."

"Now! You pwomised." The child started screaming. "I wants hot chocolate! Now! Now! Now!" The baby in the stroller chimed in with a chorus of howling.

"Now see what you've done, Madison?" Jana-Lynne scolded. "You woke Parker."

"Dids not!" Madison threw herself down on the floor. "Hot chocolate! Hot chocolate! Hot chocolate!"

"Get up off the floor," yelled Jana-Lynne. "Naughty girls don't get hot chocolate. Behave yourself."

After quickly scrawling something, Logan slipped the notebook and pen into Jana-Lynne's knapsack and whispered to Emma, "Want to make a run for it?" (from *Love, Lies and a Double Shot of Deception* by Lois Winston)

———

In the above examples, the first is boring. It tells the reader everything the reader needs to know, but who cares? When the scene is moved into dialogue, the reader is right there, hearing the clueless nanny ramble on, non-stop, both seeing and feeling the tension build as the toddler throws a tantrum and the baby wakes up. The reader experiences Emma's and Logan's reactions to the intrusion in a more visceral way that also gives a glimpse of their personalities by the way they respond to the situation.

2. Use Sensory Language

For readers to experience fully what your characters are experiencing, they need to be able to put themselves in each character's place. This is done by incorporating sensory imagery, using the five senses. Let your characters see, hear, taste, smell and touch the world around them.

A word of caution about the five senses, though. Too many writers go overboard with this. There's this *rule* that's floated around for years and has been drummed into too many writers that they must show all five senses in every scene. Nothing could be further from the truth.

Show only those senses that make sense to the scene at hand. If the heroine has just been confronted by the serial killer whose been stalking her, she's not going to notice the scent of her next-door neighbor's freshly baked apple pie wafting through her open kitchen window or hear the crunch of the Fruit Loops under her feet as she steps on the cereal her kids spilled that morning.

Example of a Poor Use of Sensory Language:

The tires of the black Jeep Cherokee squealed like trapped rats. As Marty flew from the SUV through the night, he could see the lights of the city in the far distance and hear the roar of an engine as a jet made its decent toward the airport runway. The gunman, who smelled of tobacco and Brut, started firing his Glock at him. Deadly bullets whizzed around him. Marty felt one graze his arm just as he landed face down in the half-frozen swamp. Sirens and more gunfire sounded around him.

The taste of the swamp filled his mouth. Marty reached for a shadow of something in front of him to pull himself up. It felt like rusted metal. Parts of it came off in his hand. Just as he got to his feet he was thrown backwards as a very loud and bright explosion lit up the night sky. He hit his head on something hard.

Example of Showing Using Appropriate Sensory Language:

Tires squealed. As Marty flew through the air, the gunman fired off two shots, one coming within inches of Marty's head, the other grazing his sleeve before he landed face down in a half-frozen pile of decaying muck. Blaring sirens and answering gunfire filled the air around him.

Spitting mud from his mouth, Marty lifted his head in time to see dozens of red and blue lights speed along the road in front of him. As he staggered to his feet, a deafening explosion rocked the ground, engulfing the sky in an enormous orange fireball. The force of the blast hurled him backwards into a ditch. He landed with a thud, his head striking something hard. (from *Love, Lies and a Double Shot of Deception* by Lois Winston)

In both of these examples the reader gets a sense of what's happening, but in the first there's too much extraneous information that takes away from the immediacy and realism of the scene. Both give sensory input, but the first gives too much. Notice how in the second example the reader isn't told as much but actually experiences more of Marty's plight.

3. Use Description

Description adds depth to your writing, but used unwisely, it can kill your manuscript. As with the senses, describe only that which is important to the scene and choose your descriptive words wisely. Always avoid generic adverbs and adjectives.

Example of Telling:

Emma arrived home to find the aftermath of a wild pot party that seemed to have ended rather abruptly.

Example of Showing Through the Use of Description:

Emma pushed open the unlocked front door and flipped on lights as she made her way down the central hallway toward the kitchen. Catering platters, still piled high with deli sandwiches, lined the kitchen counters. The back door stood ajar. Outside, half empty beer bottles and bowls of guacamole and salsa dotted the pool deck. Nacho chips and beer nuts littered the patio furniture and crunched beneath her feet. Still smoldering cigarette butts filled ashtrays. The sickeningly sweet aroma of pot hung in the air. (from *Love, Lies and a Double Shot of Deception* by Lois Winston)

—

Both of the examples above describe the condition of Emma's house, but the second one does so in such a way that the reader gets the sense of walking through the house with Emma and seeing for herself what Emma sees. But note what I chose to describe and what is missing from the descriptions. I describe only those things that illustrate the state of the house at the moment. The reader doesn't know the style of the house, the color of the walls, whether the hallway is carpeted or hardwood or tile, what the kitchen cabinets look like, whether the counters are marble or granite, etc. None of that matters at this point in the story or in the scene I'm writing.

4. Be Specific, Not Vague

Don't tell the reader how a character feels; show her. Don't tell the reader what a character is doing; show her.

Example of Telling:

Emma entered the Philadelphia bookstore, glad to be out of the wintry mix of snow and sleet. Classical music greeted her, and she smiled. The music reminded her of spring. She couldn't wait for sunshine and flowers. She hated February, hated winter. She looked forward to April, but then she remembered that early April often had its share of heavy snowstorms, too.

Example of Showing:

As she yanked open the door to Chapters and Verse, the "Spring Movement" of Vivaldi's *Four Seasons* greeted her. Someone had a really warped sense of humor. Or hoped the power of positive thinking could affect weather patterns. Still, the music held a reminder that the harsh realities of early February in Philadelphia would eventually give way to sunshine and flowers come late March. Maybe. Last year they'd suffered through one of their worst blizzards ever the first week in April. (from *Love, Lies and a Double Shot of Deception* by Lois Winston)

—

Both of the above paragraphs basically say the same thing, but in the first example, the reader is told things about Emma. In the second example, the reader not only *sees* Emma, she gets to know her through more specific details and less vague writing. Emma yanks open the door instead of just entering the bookstore. We learn that although she hates the weather outside and is looking forward to Spring, she's got a wry sense of humor about it, especially noting the specific music that's being played against the backdrop of a snowstorm. The reader has gotten into Emma's head and learned a lot more about her through the showing of the scene over the telling of it.

4
POOR STORYTELLING SKILLS

We've now covered the technical reasons a manuscript might be rejected. It's time to discuss the nuts and bolts of storytelling: plot and character development. Without a good plot and well-developed characters, you don't stand a chance of selling your manuscript, no matter how well you've honed your technical skills. You can have the most beautifully crafted sentences the publishing world has ever seen, but if your plot is mundane or your characters are cardboard, your chances of publication are nil.

Plot is story, and story is about what happens in a book, specifically what happens to the characters who populate that book. Characterization is what drives the people who populate the story.

Every scene in a book must do one of two things—either advance the story (plot) or tell the reader something she needs to know about the characters *at that moment* (characterization.) Plot and characterization go hand-in-hand. Even though some books are more plot-driven and others more character driven, a good book needs both.

There must be a story arc (plot) as well as a character arc (characterization.) This means the story ends in a different place from where it began, and the characters at the end of the story are not the same as they were at the beginning of the story. Both the plot and the characters must feature growth of some sort. If not, you have stagnation, and although there are some literary novels where stagnation is the theme, in commercial fiction, stagnation is a big no-no.

Heroes and heroines need to be heroic, and villains need to be despicable. However, to achieve character growth, some characters who are supposed to be heroic may not come across at their heroic best in the beginning. Why not? Because, as I said, a well-written book must show character growth. A story that begins and ends with the character having the same attitudes and in the same place emotionally and psychologically (and sometimes even physically) is not a successful story. The character needs to learn and grow from his or her experiences and the impact the other characters have had on him or her throughout the course of the story.

Another way to look at plot and characterization is to break them down in terms of the characters' internal and external goals, motivations, and conflicts. Plot deals with external goals, motivations, and conflicts. Characterization deals with internal goals, motivations, and conflicts. All characters in a novel must have both internal and external goals, motivations, and conflicts. Without them, you have melodrama, not drama.

So ask yourself the following questions:

- *Who are the characters in your story?*
- *What do they want?*
- *Why do they want what they want?*
- *What's keeping them from getting what they want?*

You must be able to answer these questions for all the major characters in your story, both the hero and heroine or protagonists, as well as any villains or antagonists. Once you break your story down in this way, you should be able to see if you've crafted a solid plot and characters that a reader will identify with on some level.

This doesn't mean that all characters have to be likeable. If a character pushes a reader's buttons, that's a well-written character. You've successfully drawn the reader into the world you've created and made the reader have feelings about the character, even if they are negative feelings. If you can't answer some of the above questions for some of the characters in your story, those are the areas of your manuscript that are weak and need work.

So let's look at goals, motivations, and conflicts in terms of plot and characters.

Goals are the "what" of a story. In terms of plot, the external goal is something concrete, something the character must do, capture, find, expose, or achieve. The plot arc will involve the protagonist's pursuit of something, whether a killer or the truth, whether a prize or a second chance, whether righting a wrong or saving the world, etc. There is often an immediacy to the goal, one that requires swift action on the part of the character. It's a black and white issue with no shades of gray. Either the character accomplishes his goal, or he doesn't. It's what drives the character and therefore drives the plot. The goal must be important enough and the character strong enough that he might have to act against his own best interests or place himself in situations of jeopardy or hardship to achieve that goal.

Whereas the external goal is physical, the internal goal is emotional. It's something that can't be measured but is driven by the external goal. It's a need for acceptance or adventure, fame or forgiveness, security or power, independence or revenge, etc. The internal goal cannot be achieved until the external goal is achieved. You can't have one without the other.

Motivation is the "why" of a story. It's what drives characters to do what they do, what defines them. The motivation might not be revealed to the reader until well into the story or even not until the end, but the author must know up front what the characters' motivations are to make those characters work for the story. Why? Because motivation is what makes readers care about characters.

External motivation is a character's back story. It's everything that has happened to the character up to that point in his or her life that puts him into a position where he must achieve his goal.

Internal motivation is the character's emotional baggage. It comes from within the character and is what gives the character depth and emotion. The plot (external motivation) must force the character to confront his emotional baggage (internal motivation.) In other words, it's what makes the character tick. Motivations must make sense to the reader and work for the character that has been created. If the reader is asked to suspend disbelief, the reason for doing so must be valid and logical. Coincidence has no place in well-crafted plots or characters.

Conflict is the "but" of the story. It's the challenge or obstacle the character must face down or overcome to achieve his or her goal. External conflict is the character up against whatever is preventing him from reaching that goal. Internal conflict is the character's battle within himself, the character flaw that he must overcome or the profound decision or sacrifice he must make to achieve his goal.

Conflict is the character's goal as opposed to the reality of his situation, his internal needs as opposed to his external goals. Often the conflict arises when one character's goals are diametrically opposed to another character's goals. If the protagonist gets what he wants, the villain doesn't get what he wants. For the heroine to achieve her goal, the hero must sacrifice his goal. Conflict is what forces character growth so that the character is a different person at the end of the book from what he or she was at the beginning of the book.

Conflict must be more than just disagreement between two characters or anger over a situation. It must be bigger than a simple weakness or fear. The stakes for not achieving the goal must be enormous, life threatening, or have impact beyond just the immediate characters.

Dialogue and Narrative

As I've mentioned previously, dialogue is one of two ways authors can show their stories. The other is active narrative (scenes where *stuff* happens.) Well-written dialogue, like well-written scenes, will do one of two things—either advance the plot and/or tell the reader something essential about the characters. Poorly written dialogue reads like filler and bores readers.

Although dialogue should sound natural and realistic, it needs to be written crisply. We all speak with lots of extraneous words and interjections. We constantly repeat ourselves. We *uhm* and *uhr* and stutter and stumble more often than not, unless we're members of Toastmasters or championship debaters. Even though these things are natural and realistic in the real world, they have no place in dialogue. Good dialogue shouldn't make the reader want to shout, "Let's get on with it. Spit it out already!"

Dialogue should also be more than just chit-chat. It should cut to the chase, not be filled with banal pleasantries.

Example of poorly written dialogue scene:

"Whatcha want, gorgeous?" said a deep, gravely voice with a heavy Brooklyn accent. He sounded like Fran Drescher on steroids.

What I'd really like was two tickets to the ballet instead of two tickets to a pro-wrestling musical extravaganza. Dave really hated the ballet as much as I really hated pro-wrestling, but I couldn't very well buy him something for his birthday that he didn't like or want, could I? Although, somehow I couldn't see him standing on line for even thirty seconds, let alone thirty minutes, to buy ballet tickets for my birthday. I ran my fingers through my mass of curly red hair and bit down on my lower lip as I wondered, did that mean I loved Dave more than he loved me?

"Hey, red, you like wanna stop like mooning over The Boulder's tight ass and like tell me whatcha want?" continued the male counterpart of Fran Drescher in a loud, booming voice. I noticed several people turn toward the ticket counter. "Like I ain't got all day, you know," he continued, his voice getting even louder.

"Uhm, Nori?" said Reese, tapping her French manicured nails on the shoulder of my taupe-colored Ralph Lauren linen cropped jacket, the one I'd bought on sale at Macy's to match the pencil skirt I was wearing. "It's your turn. You, er, want to tell the guy what you want, so we can like get out of here, maybe, and go get something to eat before our lunch hour is over?"

I hadn't realized I'd made it to the front of the line and Mr. Fran Drescher was talking to me. How absolutely embarrassing! I felt the heat quickly creeping up my neck and into my cheeks as I slowly turned to look at him. He was as wide as Fran was thin. He must have weighed three hundred pounds. He wore a skin-tight sleeveless black T-shirt with the red "AWE" logo emblazoned across his massive barrel of a chest. Muscles bulged on top of muscles on arms that were completely covered in tattoos in every imaginable color of the rainbow from his thick wrists up to his bulging shoulders. He had the thickest neck I'd ever seen, a shaved head, and an enormous gold nose ring, large enough to easily fit on my wrist, hanging down from his nostrils to his chin. I wondered how he could eat with that large thing dangling over his mouth.

He slowly drummed his beefy fingers on the counter as he leaned across, casually leering at me, as he said in a very sarcastic voice, "Any day now, doll."

———

Now, if the ticket seller is a pivotal character in the story, he needs to be mentioned in detail, but certainly there are better ways to do it. However, if this is the only time he appears in the plot (which it is,) he doesn't need to be described in such detail. And that's just the beginning of what's wrong with this dialogue passage.

Tag lines (he said, etc.) should only be used when it would be confusing to the reader not to use them. If the dialogue is between two characters, tag lines are extraneous because it's obvious who's speaking. The dialogue alternates between the two characters. If there are more than two characters in the scene, the tag line can still often be eliminated by using narrative action.

Then there's the body language which is nothing but filler. Good writing will only have a character engaged in body movements that are important enough for the point of view character to remember later. For instance, if Nori only bites down on her lower lip when she's trying to rationalize something to herself, then the lip biting is a *tell*. (Note: This is different from *telling* your story. A *tell* is an action or trait that gives insight into a character. It's often used in mystery and suspense when ferreting out the bad guys.) Maybe Nori really knows Dave isn't in love with her and has been trying to convince herself otherwise. But if the lip biting is merely a body gesture for the sake of a body gesture, it's filler and doesn't belong in the passage.

Adverbs in tag lines should be used as little as possible. Well-written dialogue should use verbs that are very descriptive to the action instead of relying on adverbs. That doesn't mean you should never use adverbs. Just make sure there's a good reason for using them. Otherwise, they become a crutch.

Finally, description for the sake of description has no place in a well-written manuscript, whether as part of a tag line, in dialogue, or in narrative. Describe only that which is important to what is happening to the characters in the scene. If the hero and heroine are running through the subway, screaming for help as they flee an ax-wielding serial killer, the heroine isn't going to notice the overflowing trash can filled with empty Starbucks cups nor the way the hero's sea green and turquoise paisley tie is flapping around his neck as they race for the exit.

Dialogue by its nature will speed up pacing. Internalization (inner thoughts, monologues) will slow pacing. There's a place for both. Good writing will have a balance, and depending on the genre, might lean more toward one than the other. But keep in mind wherever possible, you should strive to show your stories, not tell them. Too much internalization will make editors' and agents' eyes glaze over and result in a swift rejection.

So let's look at that same dialogue scene written as it appeared in the book:

"Whatcha want, gorgeous?"
Two tickets to the ballet? I smiled to myself. Dave hated the ballet as much as I hated pro-wrestling. Payback would come on *my* birthday.
"Hey, red, you wanna stop mooning over The Boulder's tight ass and tell me whatcha want? I ain't got all day."
"Nori." Reese nudged me out of my reverie.
That's when I realized I had made my way to the head of the line, and

the thick-necked guy with the nose ring and shaved head was speaking to me. (from *Talk Gertie to Me* by Lois Winston)

—

Another thing to keep in mind is that the dialogue you write must be true to the characters and period of the story. A book set in sixteenth century Scotland won't use dialogue common to nineteenth century Scotland nor twenty-first century America. A scullery maid won't speak like an aristocrat. Someone who grew up in the rural South won't speak like someone who grew up in Brooklyn. And the same is true for any internalization by those characters. What the characters say and how they say it or think it are equally important.

This doesn't mean, however, that you should be writing in the style of Chaucer or Shakespeare if your stories are set in the periods in which they wrote. Research needs to be balanced with common sense. A sprinkling of dialect goes a long way to add richness to your story without confusing the heck out of editors and agents (and ultimately readers.) You don't want editors and agents running for a dictionary – or worse yet, tossing your book aside because it's written in what seems like a foreign language.

By the same token if you're writing a story set in fourteenth century Ireland, you shouldn't be using words and phrases that didn't come into use until the twentieth century. Farmer Patrick O'Grady shouldn't be referring to his thatch roofed cottage as being as cold as the inside of a freezer if freezers aren't going to be invented for another 600 years!

5

NO ATTENTION-GRABBING OPENING HOOK

Here's a dirty little secret—most editors and agents will toss a manuscript aside after a page or two if the voice/style/story hasn't hooked them by that point. One agent has even published a book on the importance of the first five pages.

I would like to distill this down further and suggest that an author needs to hook the reader with an opening sentence. I've read thousands of submissions that open with what I can only describe as *blah* first sentences. The writer goes on to compound the problem by giving the reader several paragraphs, if not pages, of either back-story or boring description. The writer may have a fantastic story, but if he puts the editor or agent to sleep before she gets to that story, the writer has problems.

The opening of a book is meant to suck the reader into the world the author has created. Back-story can come later, trickling in to tease the reader to continue reading more, not as information dumps that pull the reader from the story. A good opening will include only the barest minimum of back-story that is essential to that moment. A good opening doesn't give editors and agents an excuse to toss aside a book. It makes them want to read more to find out what happens next.

The first sentence of a manuscript should make the reader want to read the second sentence. The hook doesn't have to be defined in the first sentence. However, that first sentence should lead you into the next sentence, and so forth until you have a paragraph that becomes a hook that grabs you as a reader and won't let go. That first paragraph should do for the first page what the first sentence did for the first paragraph, and the first page should do for the subsequent pages what the first paragraph did for the first page.

Examples of Opening Hooks:

"Times Square. Crossroads of the world," said Reese with a flourish of her arm as we exited the subway onto Forty-second Street. "And the only place in New York where you're guaranteed not to find a New Yorker." She scowled at me. "Except us." (from *Talk Gertie to Me* by Lois Winston)

~

First comes love, then comes marriage, then comes Nori pushing a baby carriage. As I stared at the words stitched on the needlepoint pillow, my cheeks burned. Leave it to my mother to transform Christmas morning into an Embarrass-Nori-Fest. Since arriving back in Ten Commandments, Iowa two days ago, I'd put up with non-stop innuendos, commentary, and sermons about my living-in-sin lifestyle and ticking biological clock. However, with the gift I'd just opened, Mom had gone too far. Way too far. (from *Elementary, My Dear Gertie* by Lois Winston)

~

"Home sweet hell," Emma muttered as she turned off the main road and guided the Mercedes down the tree-lined drive toward the house. Her estate. Not that she had any desire to return but what choice did she have? Drive around Philadelphia into the wee hours of the night? No, exhaustion precluded that option. She'd thought about checking into a hotel for the night, but she doubted the small Chestnut Hill hotel would have any available rooms this late, and she had no energy left to drive into Center City. Better to slip upstairs and hope Phillip had forgotten their earlier confrontation. (from *Love, Lies and a Double Shot of Deception* by Lois Winston)

~

I hate whiners. Always have. So I was doing my damnedest not to become one in spite of the lollapalooza of a quadruple whammy that had broadsided me last week. Not an easy task, given that one of those lollapalooza whammies had barged into my bedroom and was presently hammering her cane against my bathroom door. (from *Assault with a Deadly Glue Gun* by Lois Winston)

~

Upstairs, the front door slammed with enough force to register a five on the Richter scale. Dust dislodged from the exposed basement rafters and drifted down like polluted snow, settling over the basket of clean laundry I'd been folding. The ensuing shouting, barking, and yowling drowned out my muttered curse of choice and yanked my attention away from the now Dalmatian-spotted white wash. (from *Death by Killer Mop Doll* by Lois Winston)

~

"If that damn woman doesn't shut up, I'm going to strangle her!" (from *Revenge of the Crafty Corpse* by Lois Winston)

~

"Anastasia, I need your help." (from *Crewel Intentions* by Lois Winston)

~

"This isn't working anymore." I spoke to the ceiling, my voice controlled and emotionless. (from *Four Uncles and a Wedding* by Lois Winston, writing as Emma Carlyle)

~

The Christmas I turned six, I watched *The Nutcracker Suite* on television. During a commercial break, I bounced off the sofa, lifted my hands over my head, and twirled to a chorus of *plop-plop, fizz-fizz, oh what a relief it is.* "I want to be a ballerina," I announced loud enough to drown out the sonorous voice-over that followed the jingle. (from *Finding Hope* by Lois Winston, writing as Emma Carlyle)

~

"The trouble lies in the Y chromosome." Thea took a sip of her coffee and glared across the black Formica-topped desk at her editor, waiting to pounce on Grace if she challenged her statement. (from *Hooking Mr. Right* by Lois Winston, writing as Emma Carlyle)

~

"What made you suspect?" (from *Lost in Manhattan* by Lois Winston, writing as Emma Carlyle)

~

"No! No! No!" With a sweep of his arm Niles York rid his desk of the four

dozen eight-by-ten glossies. (from *Someone to Watch Over Me* by Lois Winston, writing as Emma Carlyle)

—

Note how even though these opening paragraphs are quite different, they all contain bits of information that pique a reader's curiosity, making her want to read more to learn the answers to questions raised in her mind. Why are two diehard New Yorkers traipsing through a part of the city most New Yorkers steer clear of? What happened earlier between Emma and Phillip that has her so scared to return to her house? What was the lollapalooza of a quadruple whammy visited upon the narrator? And so forth.

What you don't see in these openings is all sorts of needless prose. No head-to-toe descriptions of the characters. No movie camera's eye-view narrative of the settings. No weather report. Just enough information to ground the characters in a hear-and-now and give a hint of things to come.

So let's talk about description because many writers make the mistake of describing each character from head-to-toe in each scene and describing the setting from the drapes to the carpets. Yes, you need to let the reader know what characters and settings look like, but you should do this by weaving the description into the narrative and dialogue. Nothing bores a reader more than long paragraphs describing everything from the length of the heroine's hair to the color of her toenail polish when neither has anything to do with the scene at hand. (Remember, everything in a scene *must* advance the plot or tell the reader something essential she needs to know about the character *at that moment.*)

Laundry list descriptions pull the reader from the story. Pulling the reader from the story is a bad thing. It adversely affects the pacing of the book, and good pacing is something that is important to a well-written manuscript.

Sometimes the plot and conflict might not be evident in the opening of the book, but there should be enough of a tease within that opening to give the editor or agent an indication of events to come. Dialogue or narrative action is usually the best way for a writer to accomplish this. A good book will often begin by throwing the reader right into the middle of a conversation or event.

Be aware, though, that gimmickry has no place in good fiction. If you open your book with a situation that's cliché or right out of a TV sit-com, it will stand out like a neon sign. No editor or agent wants a rehash of an old *Seinfeld* or *Friends* episode.

The best hooks will draw readers into a book without them even being aware of the hook. If a hook is too obvious, all editor and agents will see is the hook and won't be drawn into your story. They may not even read past the first page.

However, when opening your book, don't think in terms of "this could never happen." Remember that truth is often stranger than fiction, and just because an author creates a situation that's unfamiliar, it doesn't mean that the situation doesn't or can't exist.

What you need to think about is whether you have created a situation that enables readers to suspend disbelief and enter the world you've created. And by *world* I don't necessarily mean a paranormal plot. The *world* is the story you've written and the characters that populate it.

So begin your books by sucking editors and agents into your world and making them not want to leave until they've come to the end of the last page. At that point they'll only want to put down the manuscript to pick up the phone to request more of the manuscript or offer you a contract.

Chapter-ending Hooks

Not only do you want to open your book with a hook, you want to end each chapter with one.

Just as you can open your book by throwing the reader into the middle of the action, you can end a chapter in much the same way. A chapter can end in the middle of a conversation or the middle of a scene, picking up in the next chapter or even several chapters later. This is a plot devise often used with great success in thrillers, mysteries, and suspense books.

I believe in few rules when it comes to writing because for every *rule* there's someone who has broken it and gone on to become a bestselling author. However, there is one rule I believe should never be broken: **Never, ever end your chapter with your characters going to sleep.**

You never want to give readers a reason to set your book aside and turn off the lights. By allowing the character to go to sleep, the author allows the reader to do the same. You should strive to keep your readers hooked and reading until they're propping their eyelids open with toothpicks because they *need* to know what happens next, and there's no way they're going to be able to sleep until they find out.

Examples of Chapter Ending Hooks:

The others grunted in agreement as I bowed my head over the pink sheet of paper. "Oh. My. God."

~

Or so I thought until Monday morning when I arrived back at the studio to find the proverbial caca had hit the proverbial fan.

~

Just as I finished reading the short note, the front door flew open.

"Freeze!"

~

As every teenage girl knows, shoeboxes make for ideal hiding places. A small stepstool stood in the middle of the walk-in closet. I pulled it over, climbed up, and reached for the highest box, one with a Bottega Veneta label. But when I lifted the lid, I didn't find a pair of Bottega Veneta shoes. Instead, I found Monica's secret.

———

The examples above are the endings of four different chapters from *Death By Killer Mop Doll*. Each one leaves the reader not knowing what happens next. When I write, my goal is to end as many chapters as possible with the reader feeling she must turn the page to find out what happens next. That should be your goal, too.

When you submit to an editor or agent, most likely you'll be asked to send the synopsis and one to three chapters or the first X number of pages (usually fifty but sometimes as few as ten or as many as 100.) I've seen many writers make the mistake of taking this request too literally, afraid that if they don't send exactly what was requested, they'll be rejected for not following *the rules* of the request.

Trust me, no editor or agent is going to reject a manuscript because you sent fifty-one pages instead of fifty. Here are some examples of what not to do:

Wanda Writer was asked to send the first thirty pages of her manuscript. Her first chapter ends on page twenty-nine. She had a great hook at the end of that first chapter, but she included the first page of the second chapter, a page that ends with a rather *blah* sentence and definitely no hook. Just because an editor or agent requested a specific number of pages, that number isn't etched in stone. Wanda should have sent twenty-nine pages instead of thirty.

Waldo Writer was asked to send the first chapter of his manuscript, but his chapters are very short, only five or six pages each. Editors and agents want to read some of your work. Since most chapters average between fifteen and twenty pages, that's what they're expecting to receive when they ask for the first chapter. So instead of sending only five pages, Waldo should have sent the first several chapters with a note of explanation in his cover letter.

Norman Novelist writes very long chapters. He's been asked to send the first twenty-five pages, but his chapter doesn't end until page thirty-two. He's got a great chapter ending hook, but he sent the first twenty-five pages, with his submission ending in the middle of a paragraph describing the contents of the hero's medicine cabinet. He should have sent the thirty-two pages.

Natasha Novelist is the most clueless of our writers. She's so afraid of doing the wrong thing that when an editor requested the first twenty-five pages of her manuscript, that's exactly what she sent, ending the submission with the last line of page twenty-five ending in mid-sentence.

The take-away here is to use common sense. Editors and agents are looking for well-written, interesting stories. Their job is to find these stories. Trust me. They're not sitting at their desks or computers looking for reasons to reject manuscripts. So don't be afraid to send a little less or a little more than they request. They'll understand why when they get to that chapter ending hook.

6
A POORLY WRITTEN QUERY LETTER

The following are excerpts from query letters I've received:

I haven't published a book before this is my first book. I'm a screenwriter (not a highly paided one) I want to get away from screenwriting and focus on books. I can expression whats in me through books more than I can in screenwriting. I get nice letters from my small group of fans who love the idea that I'm turning to writing (which I thought I would get hate mail if you like my idea please let me know. As I tell my fans. Thank you for your time of thinking of me.

~

On a stormy night Nicole Turner up stranded handsome mysterious stranger Hayden. He had all the characteristics to a perfect man.

~

The story is creatively divided into three sections: guy wins girl; guy loses girl; and guy wins girl back. Is this a novel approach, or what? Since the reading public will soon be screaming for more of Kyle and Catherine, I have already outlined two sequels to this first novel.

Obviously, I didn't request any of these writers' manuscripts.

The query is what gets you an invitation to submit your work to an editor or agent. You only have a few seconds to capture the attention of editors and agents, whether through a verbal query during an appointment at a conference or a written query sent via email or snail mail. You don't want to blow it.

Think in terms of marketing. Companies pay advertising agencies big bucks to present their products to the public in ways that will make consumers want to buy those products. But the consumer is bombarded everyday with thousands and thousands of products, a millisecond here, a few seconds there—from store shelves to roadside billboards to television and radio commercials to direct mail flyers to Internet pop-up ads.

From all that sensory input, consumers must decide which toilet bowl cleaner or underarm deodorant or dog food to purchase. Sometimes they're happy with the purchase and stick with the brand. Other times, they're dissatisfied with their choice and opt for a competitor's brand on the next shopping trip.

It's much the same with queries. From the thousands and thousands of queries editors and agents receive each year, they need to choose which ones they want to sample by requesting a partial or complete manuscript. You have all of a few seconds to make your query stand out from all the rest.

I cannot stress strongly enough how important the query letter is to your success. The main purpose of the query letter is to make the editor or agent want to read your work. As I've mentioned previously, you can't just send off a manuscript to an editor or agent. You'll find it back on your doorstep, unopened and unread, by return mail. Most editors and agents do not accept unsolicited manuscripts anymore.

The query letter is one of very few ways an unagented writer has of presenting his or her work to an editor. The only other ways are a personal recommendation from one of the editor's other authors, finaling in a writing contest that was judged by the editor, or meeting with the editor at a conference. And aside from these same few exceptions, the query letter is the only way to snag an agent's attention.

The query is broken up into four parts:

- nuts and bolts
- the hook
- the blurb
- author information

First and foremost, you want to write a query letter that's about the book. Include information which will pique editors' and agents' interest about the specific work you're asking them to read. That's where the hook, the blurb, and the nuts and bolts come in.

Don't fill the query letter with all sorts of biographical facts about yourself and not enough about your book. Agents and editors are interested in one thing: your writing. They don't want to know that you're the PTA president or editor of your church newsletter. Include only that information about yourself that has bearing on your book. However, if you have a platform, do mention it.

Platform is very important these days. Publishers look favorably upon authors with platform because platform helps sell books. Having a platform means that you have a built-in audience for your books. If you write a famous blog with millions of hits a day or you're a movie star or a well-known athlete, you have a platform. For us lesser mortals, if your "day job" is related to the book (i.e. you're a doctor who writes medical thrillers), that's your platform, and you should mention it. If your education has some bearing on your writing, either because it's in creative writing or because it's in a field that's closely related to the plot or setting of your book, include it.

The Nuts and Bolts

Your query should be in the form of a standard business letter with letterhead, date, recipient's address, salutation, body of letter, closing, and signature. Keep your query letter to one page. Tighten it until it squeaks. But make sure it contains *all* pertinent information including the title, genre and word count. Make sure the letterhead includes your name, address, telephone, email, and website and blog URL's.

Many editors and agents will check out a writer's cyberspace presence before deciding whether to request a manuscript. The website and/or blog offers them additional information that the writer can't cram into a one-page query letter and shows editors and agents how serious a writer the person is.

Editors and agents will also Google you, as will others at the publishing house when they're considering offering you a contract. So make sure that anything floating around the Internet presents you as a serious, mature, professional person. Those Facebook photos of drunken partying down in Cabo during spring break or political diatribes on YouTube can and will come back to haunt you years later in more ways than you can imagine.

Email queries should contain *all* the same information as above although the letterhead information generally comes at the end of the email instead of at the beginning.

Keep the query letter professional and business-like. Don't tell editors and agents how wonderful your book is or that your great-aunt Mabel thinks it will be a bestseller unless Great-aunt Mabel happens to be a fiction editor or an agent. And in that case, you really don't need to be writing a query letter, do you? Also, don't write to editors and agents as if they're your best friends.

Send as much material as the guidelines allow, but even if the guidelines don't mention it, include the first two or three pages of the manuscript. This is a gamble, but it can pay off, especially if your query letter hasn't grabbed the attention of the editor or agent. The pages will show your style, voice, and skill.

Conversely, many writers can knock out a fabulous query letter, but when the actual pages arrive, they receive an immediate rejection. It's the pages that ultimately sell you as a potential client or author, not the query letter, but a well-written query letter is your foot in the door.

Carefully compose your query letter. Don't use run-on sentences, and make sure you check for grammatical errors. If you write run-on sentences full of grammatical errors, you're not going to receive a request, no matter how innovative and exciting your book sounds. Proofread for spelling errors and typos. If your one-page letter is laden with typos, the editor is going to assume the same will be true for your four-hundred-page manuscript. And don't forget to use Spell Check! You'd be surprised how many people don't. If you're sending an e-query, set your email so that it automatically spell checks your post before it's sent, but don't set it to automatically correct the spelling. That can lead to all sorts of unintentional typos.

The Hook

Some books and articles suggest beginning a query with the pertinent information about the book—the genre and word count. I disagree. Nothing is more boring than reading a query that begins, "My name is Alice Author and I've written a 100,000-word paranormal romance novel set in a small town in Iowa." If you have a high concept or attention-grabbing sentence that describes your book, beginning your query with it will instantly grab the attention of the editor or agent. Genre and word count can come later.

Examples of Query Letter Opening Sentences That Work:

What if Arthur and Guinevere had built Hogwarts? (opening sentence of a query for a young adult fantasy series)

~

Lucy and Ethel do Africa. That's the rollicking premise behind... (beginning of a query for a memoir about a trip to Africa)

~

Tripp and Trina Light, sixteen-year-old twins, never expected to find themselves smack in the middle of a zombie apocalypse when their parents left them home alone for the weekend. (opening sentence of a query for *Dead (a Lot)*, a humorous young adult horror novel by Howard Odentz.)

—

As you can see from the examples above, query opening sentences can be short and pithy, long and complex, or somewhere in-between. Sometimes the type of book will determine the best way to construct that opening sentence.

What's important is that you create an opening that will make the editor or agent want to read more of the query and ultimately request a partial or full manuscript.

State any information about your previous experience with the agent or editor (if any,) such as previous requests and/or meetings (even casual ones) or referrals from another author who works with that editor or agent, whether she judged a writing contest where you finaled, whether she rejected an earlier manuscript but encouraged you to contact her if you had another, etc.

Don't compare your writing to an author the editor or agent already handles. Why would she want you when she already has her? You don't want to position yourself as a pale imitator. However, what you can do is state that your book will appeal to fans of Norman Novelist and Agnes Author. Those few simple words will convey a ton of meaning to editors and agents. They'll know immediately that you've studied the marketplace and will also give them a sense of your style and voice.

Give a short plot summary similar to what you'd find on back cover copy. State where and when the book is set. Tell who the main characters are. You'd be surprised how many authors forget to include these important details.

State if the book is the first in a planned series and mention your plans for the other books in the series, but emphasize that the book has a satisfying ending and would work as a stand-alone.

Include a very brief summary of other completed manuscripts if you have any.

Try to echo your writing voice in your query. The tone in the paragraph about your plot should echo your writing voice; it should sound like the ideal back cover copy for the book.

If you have an author quote, include it (but first ask the author for permission.) Don't mention contest wins or writing awards unless they're major ones such as Romance Writers of America's Golden Heart Award or a publisher sponsored contest. Mention if you're a member of any national writing organizations, but don't list the various chapters of those organizations or that you belong to a critique group.

If the query is going to an agent, list any editors who currently have the manuscript and any who have already rejected it. It's important to be honest with the agent. If the book has already been shopped around and rejected everywhere by you or another agent, the agent you're querying isn't going to be able to change editors' minds. And if she signs you, she's going to be seriously annoyed when she discovers you've wasted her time.

Don't send cover art, illustrations, or gifts. Don't ask editors and agents to purchase your other books or anything else, like the person who sent this query letter:

If you buy one of my books off of Amazon, or barnesandnoble.com, just to check it out, I will give you FREE, either 10 brand new assorted adult DVD's if you want, or any sexy clothing item up to $20 for FREE from my website, just send me the book back, and include a note of what you are trading for, even exchange. Or just tell me what you want, to get you to look at one of my books, I will do just about anything. Thank you very much.

Finally, end your letter with a brief, professional, courteous closing.

If you follow these simple rules, you'll wind up with a well-written query letter that just might solicit a request from the editors and agents.

Sample Query Letter That Resulted in a Multi-book Contract:

Here's a little secret: even agents write query letters. We write them to editors we think might be a good fit for books we're trying to sell. Below is a query letter I wrote that resulted in a 3-book deal for my client.

Dear Edith Editor,

What if Scott Turow's *One L* met Cassandra Clare's Mortal Instruments series?

In a post-Apocalyptic world, humans, angels, and the descendents of Lucifer's army all live together. Life remains much as it did prior to Armageddon. People get married, have babies, pay their taxes. The only difference is that now the demons and their Maegesters are in charge.

Reluctant Maegester Noon Onyx has been accepted into the prestigious St. Lucifer's Law School where her mother hopes she'll be trained as a Demon Lawyer. Noon views as a curse her ability to destroy things by thought or touch. Her dream is to become a Mederi, a grower of gardens and healer of people.

Peter Aster, Noon's best friend, is an Angel spellcaster who thinks he has the answer to Noon's predicament – an ancient lost spell that can turn Noon into the Mederi she yearns to be. Only one person stands in the way of Noon's dream – Ari Carmine, a powerful and charismatic Maegester fascinated by Noon's fiery side.

Dark Light of Day by Jill Archer is a 110,000-word urban fantasy that would appeal to fans of Kat Richardson's Greywalker Series, Carrie Vaughn's Kitty and the Midnight Hour Series, and Cassandra Claire's Mortal Instruments Series. The author practiced law for ten years and has taught law as an adjunct professor. This knowledge and experience infuse her manuscript with richness and credibility. Although a satisfying read in and of itself, the author envisions **Dark Light of Day** as the first of a series and has already begun work on a follow-up book.

May I email you the manuscript and synopsis?

Sincerely,
Lois Winston
Ashley Grayson Literary Agency

7

A POORLY WRITTEN SYNOPSIS

Most writers, whether published or unpublished, hate writing a synopsis. Unfortunately, the sad fact of the publishing world is that you must be able to write a good synopsis. You not only need a synopsis to get published, you need a synopsis to keep getting published because once published, you'll be lucky enough to sell on partial. And that means the first three chapters *plus* a synopsis.

A synopsis will help sell an agent or editor on your book. When you submit to agents and editors, they'll most likely begin by reading the first few pages of your manuscript. If they like the opening, they'll go on to read a few chapters. If they're still loving your work at that point, they'll look at the synopsis to see if you've got all your little duckies lined up in their proper rows. Once they've determined from the synopsis that you've covered all the essential character GMC and have a great story arc and resolution, they'll go back and finish reading the manuscript. Or if they've only requested a partial, they'll ask for the remainder of the manuscript.

The agent also uses the synopsis to pitch your book to editors, and the editor uses the synopsis to pitch the book to the editorial board. Once the book sells, the synopsis will also be used by the marketing department, the publicity department, and the cover artist. So the synopsis is a very important part of an author's work, and you need to make sure yours clearly conveys your book to editors and agents. A poorly written synopsis often leads to a rejection. A well-written synopsis (along with well-written pages) often leads to an offer of representation or a sale.

A synopsis is always written in present tense, usually in third person. However, if you've written a first-person book, you may choose to write your synopsis in first person. That's perfectly acceptable.

Avoid inserting passages from the manuscript into the synopsis. Don't use dialogue, and don't go into long descriptive paragraphs about what your characters look like.

A synopsis is *not* a chapter by chapter outline of what happens in your book. It shouldn't read like a junior high school book report.

Most editors and agents want a synopsis between one and ten pages. Some request a page of synopsis for every ten thousand words of the manuscript. However, no matter how long your synopsis, it must be concise and free of unimportant details. The synopsis should give the story arc, touching on all major plot points, as well as the resolution of the story and all conflicts. A synopsis that ends with the author telling the editor to buy the book if she wants to learn what happens is not a synopsis any editor wants to see.

The synopsis should also give the internal and externals goals, motivations, and conflicts of all the major characters in the book. Note, I said *major* characters—the characters the story is about. Secondary characters should be kept to a minimum in a synopsis and to avoid confusion should be referred to by description rather than name (the neighbor, the sister, the boss, etc.) whenever possible. However, there are exceptions to this. For instance, a mystery synopsis should include all the suspects.

For each of the major characters the following questions should be answered: What does the character want (both internally and externally)? Why does he want it? What's keeping him from getting it? Does he get what he wants in the end? How is the conflict resolved?

Remember how I stated earlier that the main characters in your book must experience emotional growth? That the book should never end with the characters in the same place they were at the beginning of the book? The synopsis must include this emotional growth and transformation and how and why it occurred.

Finally, a synopsis should not be a dry read. The best synopses are ones in which the authors have been able to instill the voice used in their manuscripts into their synopses.

There are many books available and articles on the Internet that will help you learn to write a synopsis. There are also online workshops devoted strictly to synopsis writing. Take advantage of them if you need help. Suck it up and work on your synopsis writing. Once you master synopsis writing, you'll be glad you did. And if I haven't given you enough incentive, think about this: There are authors who have signed mega-deals based on synopsis alone, without ever writing the first sentence of the book.

Synopsis Format

The synopsis is formatted exactly like a manuscript with the following exceptions:

- There is no need to begin 1/3 - 1/2 down the page the way you would at the beginning of a chapter.

- Include the word **synopsis**, title of the book, and the author's name centered at the beginning of the synopsis.

- Include the word **synopsis** in the header with the author's name, title of the manuscript, and page count.

- The first time a character is named, type the name all in caps.

Sample Synopsis:

Synopsis
TALK GERTIE TO ME
by Lois Winston

The worst day of HONORA STEDWORTH's life begins like any other spring day in New York City—hectic but normal. It deteriorates rapidly. Nori's initial mistake is grabbing a bite of lunch from a street vendor. First, she burns the roof of her mouth on the chicken burrito. Five minutes later, she's covered head to toe when a limo speeds through a puddle of sludge.

Knowing she can't go back to work looking as she does, she heads for her boyfriend's apartment to clean up and change into fresh clothes. Luckily, she has a key. Unfortunately, he and her best friend have decided to lunch in his Jacuzzi.
Could life get any worse? Nori discovers it most certainly can when she arrives home to find her mother camped out at her apartment door.

CONSTANCE STEDWORTH is suffering from middle-aged melt-down. She feels useless and worthless. Her only identity is as a wife and mother, but her husband, the mayor, is constantly occupied with town business, and her daughter is halfway across the country. If only Nori would come to her senses and marry town mortician and most eligible bachelor, EUGENE DRAYMORE, Mom would have grandchildren to give her life purpose. To that end, she has traveled to New York with a plan to bring Nori home.

Nori moved half-way across the country to escape the restrictive small-town mentality of her family. Mayor for as long as Nori can remember, EARNEST STEDWORTH oversees his own little fiefdom, commanding unswerving respect from all three thousand residents of Ten Commandments, Iowa.

Up until several hours ago, Nori thought she had created a successful, fulfilling life for herself outside the confines of Ten Commandments. She had a satisfying career, a best friend, and a devoted lover. Now her mother is back trying to run her life, her closest friend turns out to be a Judas, and her boyfriend turns out to be a two-timing louse.

When Nori calls her office, she learns the Internet company she works for has filed for bankruptcy. She has no savings, no job, and a shopaholic mother who in one day manages to max out Nori's credit card.

Her tiny apartment no longer her own, Nori escapes as often as possible to a neighborhood coffeehouse where she spends hours nursing a single cup of latte, even if she really can't afford it. In-between working on her résumé and searching job boards she hammers out revenge fantasies on her laptop.

Nori resurrects GERTIE, the alter ego of her adolescence, an imaginary companion created by a lonely child. However, like Nori, Gertie has grown up. Now, instead of helping Nori combat the twelve-year-old bullies and domineering relatives of Ten Commandments, Gertie takes on the inequities of life in the Big Apple as seen through Nori's eyes. Gertie is everything Nori feels she isn't. She fights back instead of tucking tail and running away or giving in to avoid a scene. At least on paper.

When Nori inadvertently grabs the wrong laptop one afternoon, her tongue-in-cheek essays wind up in the hands of MACKENZIE RANDOLPH, station manager for WBAT—Big Apple Talk Radio. Nori is furious when she discovers Mac has read her files, but her anger quickly dissipates when he offers her a daily five-minute on-air segment.

WBAT is suffering from low ratings. Mac is in jeopardy of losing his job. He sees Nori's biting humor as the infusion the station needs to draw new listeners. Nori agrees to his offer. Her one demand is that he keeps her identity a secret. She has enough problems with her parents. She can't imagine the repercussions if her uncensored fantasies hit the airwaves and somehow find their way back to Iowa.

Meanwhile, Mom has struck up a friendship with Nori's neighbor, successful entrepreneur HYMAN PERTH. Hy takes an interest in Mom's crafts, especially her quirky belly button castings portraits. He soon has her convinced he can turn her into the next Martha Stewart.

Through his vast network of connections, Hy makes arrangements for Mom's crafts to be marketed in some of the finest New York department stores and boutiques. Before a single item is on the shelves, the marketing blitz begins, and Mom becomes the belly button portrait artist to the stars. When Hy secures her a guest appearance on *Late Show*, Mom casts Mel Gibson's navel in front of sixty million viewers.

Nori doesn't trust her neighbor. She can't understand why a sophisticated New Yorker would want to manufacture Mom's crafts. Suspecting he's actually out to con her naïve mother, Nori debates calling her father.

Nori and her father have spoken little since she came to New York—the aftermath of her only act of defiance against him. Instead of accepting both the teaching position he had secured for her after college and Eugene, the man he and her mother hand-selected as her husband, Nori took off to prove she could succeed on her own.

Dad nurses a grudge over her rejection of his choices for her. In his eyes, he knows what's best for his little girl. If she contacts him, Nori will have to admit her failure. She weighs her father's smug I-told-you-so attitude against living a moment longer with her out-of-control mother, swallows her pride, and places the call.

Little does Nori realize she has played right into her mother's hands. Mom never intended to leave her husband permanently. Her act was all a ploy to achieve her double goal of convincing Nori to come home and getting Earnest to pay more attention to her. She fully expects Earnest to come running to her rescue—even if she doesn't believe she needs rescuing.

Once Nori's daily spots on WBAT air, she becomes the talk of the city. Each day she waxes acerbic on some frustration with which millions in her listening audience can relate. Her segment, *Gertie Gets Even*, is repeated several times throughout the day. Within a week, Mac offers her an hour-long call-in show, and Nori becomes a hip radio version of Dear Abby, dispensing twenty-first century advice to her callers.

Meanwhile, Dad arrives in New York. To Nori's horror, he comes with a dual purpose—to reclaim his wife, whom he believes has been seduced and corrupted by Nori's nefarious neighbor, and convince Nori to come home. To aid him in his mission, he has enlisted the help of Eugene, who is in New York for a morticians' conference.

Thanks to Hy, for the first time in her life, Connie feels she's a somebody, rather than an extension of her husband and daughter. Not wanting to give up her new-found celebrity, she refuses to return to her old life in Ten Commandments. This pronouncement horrifies both her husband and her daughter. Dad announces he has no intentions of leaving New York without his wife. He will stay in New York until Connie comes to her senses and agrees to return to Ten Commandments where she belongs.

Bedlam ensues.

Nori has never heard her parents raise their voices at each other. She can't remember hearing them have so much as a disagreement, let alone a fight. In the past, Mom always deferred to Dad—in everything. With Nori and Eugene looking on in horror, Mom makes up for nearly thirty years of repressed anger.

As a timid adolescent, Nori used Gertie as an escape. Gertie's adult incarnation has become a reflection of a Nori who is now her own woman. For the first time in her life she is confident of her own worth as a person and her own decisions regarding her life.

Although she made some mistakes along the way, initially trading a controlling family for a manipulative boyfriend and being so desperate for a best friend that she walked head-first into a toxic relationship, she has grown from those experiences.

Over the past several weeks, Mac and Nori have built a friendship that supersedes any relationship she has ever experienced. His faith in her makes her realize that she and Gertie are one in the same. She walks out in the middle of her parents' altercation and meets up with Mac. Although she has sworn to both Gertie and herself that she won't sleep with her boss, she and Mac wind up spending the night together.

Nori is certain she's in love but insists on taking things slowly—at least in all areas other than sex. Mac doesn't mind her live-for-the-moment attitude. He knows down the road they'll be giving Connie those grandbabies she wants, even if Connie is convinced he's spoiling her plans for Nori and Eugene.

The next morning, Nori returns home to change her clothes. Late for her show, she runs out before her parents can interrogate her. Eugene, who has arrived at the apartment, follows her. He's finally mustered the courage to admit the secret he's hidden from everyone in Ten Commandments: he's gay.

When Nori arrives at work, she discovers Mac's dedication to her is jeopardizing his job. By honoring his agreement to keep her identity secret, he's defied the station's owners who want an aggressive advertising campaign centered around Nori. Mac may lose his job due to her lack of backbone. She decides to give both her parents and Ten Commandments a giant kick into the twenty-first century and insists Mac launch the campaign.

Back at Nori's apartment, Mom convinces Dad that she isn't a fallen woman and has never loved anyone but him. Her relationship with Hy is strictly business. Although she initially only wanted Dad to pay attention to her, she's enjoying herself too much to give up her newly launched career.

Dad's regressive attitudes nearly jeopardized his marriage. After a teary reconciliation, they agree to find a compromise. When Eugene arrives and admits his homosexuality, Mom and Dad realize their well-meaning interference could have forced Nori and Eugene into a disastrous situation.

Mom and Dad seek Nori out at the station and apologize for trying to control her life. Neither has ever wanted anything but the best for her. Although they both still have misgivings about her life in New York, they see that she is truly happy. Dad admires his daughter's backbone and the courage it took to stand up to him. Mom decides to find a way to accept Mac now that her dream of a Stedworth/Draymore union is dead.

Earnest eventually overcomes his paranoia and accepts Hy as Connie's business partner and nothing more. Because he loves his wife, he has no choice but to accept the "new" Connie. Connie agrees to establish her budding empire back in Ten Commandments where Earnest will step down as mayor to manage day-to-day operations of Connie Stedworth

Enterprises. Connie will be free to handle the creative end of the business, leaving marketing for Hy to run from New York.

8

SHE'S JUST NOT THAT INTO YOU(R) VOICE/STYLE

Even though your manuscript is technically flawless, your plot interesting, your characters fully developed, your manuscript keeps receiving rejections. Why? You've done everything right. The offers should be coming in left and right. Instead, you're told the voice didn't grab the editor or agent or the style of the writing fell flat or wasn't tight enough.

Voice and style are very subjective. What appeals to one editor or agent might not appeal to another. All you need do is compare different authors within the same sub-genre to see this. For example, look at all the paranormal books about vampires. Some are dark and erotic; others are light and humorous. You can see this distinction just by looking at the book covers. Readers will gravitate toward one or the other, depending on how they prefer their vampires served up. The authors of these books have developed voices that complement their writing styles. If you switched out the voice of a dark, erotic author for that of a light, humorous author, you'd have two authors who probably would never sell. Voice must match style.

But remember what I said above: Voice and style are very subjective. If your voice isn't right for one editor or agent, it might be exactly what another loves.

That's the thing with subjectivity. It's all based on personal preference and taste.

Genre often dictates writing style. For example, I recently read an historical fiction manuscript with a concept I loved. I found the story intriguing, especially since it was based on fact and the author had done extensive research into the time period. The writing was clean, crisp, well-paced, and entertaining. However, in the end, I rejected the manuscript. Why? Because the author's voice didn't match the genre and time period of her manuscript. As I read, I kept hearing contemporary characters in my head, not the sixteenth century characters of her story. I hated having to reject that book, but I knew I wouldn't be able to sell it as it was written.

Unfortunately, voice is something a writer either has or doesn't have. Voice is something writers can develop over time if they're lucky, but voice can't be taught. I can't give you a list of rules to follow that will develop a voice if you don't yet have one.

However, a writer can improve the style of her writing in several ways. First, study the genre you've chosen for your manuscript. Different genres dictate different styles of prose. The style of Janet Evanovich's Stephanie Plum books wouldn't work for Philippa Gregory's series of historical novels about the court of Tudor England nor the dystopian young adult fiction of Suzanne Collins. If your style doesn't work with your chosen genre, you either need to switch genres or change your style.

If the style isn't right for any genre, then chances are the writing isn't tight enough. This is a common reason cited on rejection letters. Too many authors pad their writing, bogging it down with unnecessarily long, repetitive passages filled with convoluted sentences, paragraph after paragraph of filler, and dialogue that goes nowhere. Editors and agents want tightly crafted manuscripts.

Write Tight(ly)

You've gotten to the end of your manuscript. What a sense of accomplishment to type THE END. After months or maybe years of labor, your baby is ready to leave its cozy Microsoft or Apple womb and fly off to that A-List of agents and/or editors.

Then the rejection letters start arriving, and each one mentions that the writing isn't "tight" enough. You scratch your head. What does that mean? Simply stated, it means you're verbose. You ramble and repeat and use too many words to get your point across.

So before you start sending baby out into the world, you want to make sure she's not a porker bloated by excess wordage that drags down your pacing and bores the very people you want to impress. You want your manuscript lean, your writing crisp and succinct, to stand out and catch the eye of that A-list editor or agent.

Another thing to keep in mind: Publishers want shorter novels these days. Longer books cost more to print and ship. Most novels used to be a minimum of 100,000 words. Now editors are looking for book that are a maximum of 100,000 words and ideally somewhere between 75,000 and 95,000 words. There are still those mega-tomes that are published, but there are fewer and fewer of them, and publishers will more often only publish them if they've been written by well-established authors with a huge following.

So if you need to put your baby on a word diet to shed that excess word weight, here's how you do it:

The Bloated Manuscript Diet

1. Reread your manuscript. Is every scene essential to the plot or the goals, motivations, and conflicts of your characters? Does each scene advance the plot or tell the reader something she needs to know about the characters? If not, the scene is filler, and you need to get rid of it. Each scene must serve a

purpose. No purpose? No scene.

2. Repeat Step 1 for all dialogue. If the dialogue is nothing but chit-chat, delete it.

3. Do a search of "ly" words. Wherever possible, substitute a more active, descriptive verb to replace your existing verb and the adverb that modifies it.

- Joe walked purposefully across the room.

- Joe **strode** across the room.

4. Although every word in the English language can be used in your manuscripts, there are some words that are overused by authors and should either be avoided altogether or used as little as possible. For most of these words a more descriptive noun, adjective, or verb would go a long way to improving the sentence. Whenever possible, go for specific over generic.

5. Instead of using many adjectives to describe a noun, use one all-encompassing adjective or a more descriptive noun.

- Elizabeth grew up in an old, large house with twenty rooms.

- Elizabeth grew up in a Victorian mansion.

6. Say it once, then move on. It's not necessary to repeat an idea or image in different words in the next sentence, the next paragraph, or on the next page.

- A kettledrum pounded in Elizabeth's head. Her temples throbbed. Her skull pulsated with pain.

You've said all you need to say with the first sentence. If a drum is pounding in her head, it's understood that her temples would throb, and she'd be in pain. Why is it necessary to reiterate the obvious? You don't need to beat your reader over the head. She's intelligent enough to "get it" the first time she reads it, and that goes for editors and agents, too.

7. Identify needless words and eliminate them. Every writer has at least one or two pet word she overuses. **Just** is a major culprit, but there are others. Search your manuscript for these needless words and get rid of them.

8. Avoid laundry list descriptions by substituting more descriptive nouns and adjectives.

- Joe wore a blue and green plaid threadbare shirt with missing buttons and a pair of frayed black jeans torn below the knees.

- Joe wore Salvation Army rejects.

Both sentences convey a similar image, but the second one does so without going into unnecessary minute detail and makes for a more interesting sentence.

9. Do a search for **was**. Wherever it's linked with an **ing** verb, omit the **was** and change the tense of the verb.

- Elizabeth was walking down the street.

- Elizabeth walked down the street.

10. Choose more descriptive verbs and omit the additional words that enhance the verb.

- Joe walked with a swaggering gait down the street.

- Joe swaggered down the street.

11. Omit extraneous tag lines. If it's obvious which character is speaking, a tag line is unnecessary. Use tag lines only when there are three or more characters taking part in the dialogue scene.

12. Show, don't tell. Wherever possible, you want to "show" your story through dialogue and active narrative, rather than "telling" the story.

13. Let your characters' words convey their emotion, not the tag line. Also, keep to the unobtrusive **said** in tags. You can't **grimace**, **laugh** or **sigh** dialogue. The character can grimace, laugh, or sigh before or afterward but not while speaking. And don't overdo it. It grows old very quickly and will grate on the nerves of editors and agents.

14. Avoid non-specific words like **it** and **thing**.

15. Describe body movements only when they're essential to the scene. Don't break up dialogue every other sentence by having your characters shrug, nod, drum their fingers, or move in any way just for the sake of moving. This is another form of filler.

16. Don't fill dialogue with interjections. We might have the bad habit of peppering our speech with **well** and **like**, **uhm** and **er**, but having a character constantly adding those words makes for lousy dialogue.

Did you notice how many of these "dieting" tips are items I covered in earlier chapters?

If you find you can't be objective about your voice and style (and many of us can't), ask someone who can give your work an objective read. Remember, though, unless they're published authors in their own right, most family members and BFFs don't fall into the objective category. They'll either love every word you write because they love you, or they'll be overly critical because they're jealous. In most cases, it's best to ask a published author or if you have the discretionary income, use the services of a reputable freelance editor.

9
POOR TIMING

Sometimes life just sucks, and there's not much you can do if your manuscript ends up on the wrong editor's desk on the wrong day. In this instance, I'm not referring to an editor who doesn't buy what you've written. We've already discussed that back at the beginning of this book. I'm talking about plain old bad timing and the "We're All Human" factor. Editors and agents are neither automatons nor gods. We're human beings with human foibles, and sometimes, even though we work hard not to, we do allow our personal lives to horn in on our professional lives.

So what follows are some other reasons why you may have received that rejection letter, even if you've written a publishable book.

1. The editor recently purchased a book with a similar plot or has a book with a similar plot due to release soon.

2. The publisher had a book with a similar plot or similar characters that sold poorly, and all the editors at this particular publishing house are shying away from buying these types of books. (Something to keep in mind—editors advance up the editorial food chain by discovering talented authors whose books make money for the publisher. It's all about the bottom line.)

3. There is already a glut on the market of the type of book you've written. That's why it's so important not to follow trends. Unless you write incredibly fast, by the time you recognize a trend and write a book to that trend, the trend will most likely be on the downside. Publishers will have more than enough inventory of those books and won't be buying any more except from their well-established authors who are already writing to that trend.

Ever notice that some authors are still selling chick lit, even though everyone says chick lit is dead? That's because these were the authors on the forefront of the trend, and the publishers know people will still buy their books. But if you're just trying to break into the chick lit market, your chances of selling won't be very good. Same thing for vampire books. Personally, my eyes glaze over when I see yet another query about a vampire book. Every editor I've spoken to feels the same way. Vampire books are still selling, but the publishers are only interested in buying from established authors when it comes to vampire books. If you really, really want to write chick lit or vampire books or any other over-saturated trend, you'd better be sure you've come up with a unique twist that no one else has thought of.

4. The editor is still buying the type of books you write but not quite what you've written. Perhaps she's looking for older heroines or multi-cultural heroines to round out her list. Or she needs historicals set in countries other than Scotland, England, and Ireland. Or shape-shifter books are really doing well for her, but she's overstocked on werewolf titles.

5. The editor loved the book and wanted to buy it, but she couldn't convince her senior editor or the editorial review board. This happens more often than most people realize because rarely will the editor state this reason in her rejection letter. Also, very few editors in publishing have the seniority to offer a contract on their own. Others up the ladder have to sign off on the deal.

6. You had the misfortune of landing on her desk on the worst day of her life. Maybe her boyfriend just dumped her for Barbie Boob Job, and the heroine of your book is named Barbie. Maybe she woke up this morning to find her cat had barfed a hairball all over the $400 pair of Manolos she's still paying off on

her maxed-out credit card. Maybe she partied too hard the night before, drank one too many Appletinis, and woke this morning to find a stranger in her bed. Maybe she broke a nail taking the binder clip off your submission and she'd just had her nails done during her lunch hour. Maybe that morning she was reamed by her senior editor for something she did or didn't do. Maybe she has PMS or is menopausal. Maybe she had a fight with her mother the night before or her husband that morning. Maybe her kids were being uncooperative at breakfast, and she was late for work and missed an important meeting. Or maybe she's just having a bad hair day.

The point is, we all get in moods and often take those moods out on others, whether we're justified in doing so or not. You will never know whether your manuscript was rejected for one of these reasons. However, chances are, if you've been submitting for any length of time, you did have the misfortune to score a rejection letter that had nothing to do with the quality of your writing, your story, or the characters you've crafted. Caca happens. All you can do is dust yourself off and keep submitting. If your book is as good as you believe it is, you'll eventually find a home for it.

And don't think these rejections only happen to unpublished authors. I recently received a rejection where the editor stated, "The author has a really nice and accessible voice and she's created appealing characters, but I'm sorry to say I didn't find myself falling in love with the writing."

Now wouldn't you think that if an editor said she thought you had a "really nice and accessible voice" that it meant she liked your writing? As I said at the beginning of this chapter, sometimes life just sucks.

10
THE CLUELESS WRITER

Finally, I'd like to discuss two separate issues that both fall under the heading of Clueless Writer. I struggled for a politically correct way to say this, but frankly, I couldn't come up with anything that would encompass both issues other than the "clueless" moniker. So please don't take offense. I'm using the term with tongue firmly planted in cheek. I doubt there isn't an author out there who hasn't been clueless at one time or another, and I count myself in that group.

Many times, a writer is rejected because she doesn't have a completed manuscript. Although it rarely happens, sometimes an unpublished author will sell on a partial. When this occurs, it's most often because she's previously completed other manuscripts that didn't sell for reasons having nothing to do with the quality of the writing. The editors knew that the author was capable of finishing a book in a timely manner and may even have wanted to buy one of the other manuscripts but couldn't.

That's the key. No editor is going to take a chance on an unknown quantity, and a writer who hasn't finished a manuscript is an unknown quantity. Some people can write a book in three months. Others take three years. Or more. I know many writers who are still tinkering with the first three chapters of the same book for going on ten years and have yet to finish a single book.

When an editor makes an offer to purchase a manuscript, she needs to know that the author will be able to deliver the completed manuscript by a certain date spelled out in the contract. Too much time, money, and effort will have already been spent on the author by that date, and if the author doesn't deliver, the editor has a problem. A huge problem. That's why most editors won't make an offer on an unfinished book by an unpublished writer. They can't take the chance that something might go wrong.

So when the editor or agent requests the complete manuscript based on a query or partial she's read and is told the manuscript is not yet finished, she'll tell the writer to contact her again when the manuscript is finished. But stuff often happens in the interim. Depending on how long it takes the writer to finish the manuscript, the agent or editor may no longer be interested in the book. Maybe the agent has signed another client who writes something very similar. Or the editor may have moved to another job within the publishing house or to another publisher and is no longer acquiring such books. Or maybe the agent has retired. The editor may have left publishing or taken an extended maternity leave. Like I said, stuff happens.

Conversely, I know many authors who have sold by being in the right place at the right time because stuff happens. An author on deadline falls ill or for some other reason can't deliver her book by deadline. The editor winds up with a hole in her list for that month. It just so happens that she was judging a contest recently and requested the complete manuscript of the person she chose as the winner. This lucky writer had a finished manuscript to send. The manuscript was sitting on the editor's shelf, waiting for a time when she could read it. The editor pulls the manuscript off the shelf, reads it, and calls the writer to make an offer. True story.

Timing is everything. Had the author not had a complete manuscript to send the editor, the story would have had a different ending. Unfortunately, this was the one and only book this author sold. She had spent so many years perfecting that one manuscript that she had nothing else of equal quality to offer the editor for her option book. More than twenty years later, that author still hasn't sold another book.

The other reason under the "clueless" heading is the writer's inability to recognize an opportunity when she receives one. Editors and agents are extremely busy individuals. They juggle many duties on a daily basis and read thousands and thousands of queries each year. If an editor or agent takes the time to write you a detailed, personal rejection letter rather than sending a two-sentence form rejection, that's an opportunity that too many writers don't recognize.

When agents and editors take the time to list the reasons why they're rejecting your book, they're telling you that your book has merit. They're leaving the door open for a resubmission. Take the time to study what's spelled out in the rejection letter. Revise your manuscript based on those comments. The editors and agents won't bother making such comments if they don't see potential in your work. They're too busy to spend time on something they know they'd never buy or represent.

So if you get one of those rejection letters, don't toss it in with the others. Grab hold of the opportunity to improve your manuscript and resubmit it. They're expecting that you will. Just don't take too long. The window of opportunity is a limited one for the very reasons I mentioned above.

ABOUT THE AUTHOR

Lois Winston is a critically acclaimed *USA Today* and Amazon bestselling and award-winning author and a retired literary agent whose clients have included authors of urban fantasy, young adult, new adult, mystery, women's fiction, horror, and romance. Lois began her career in publishing in 2006 with the release of her humorous women's fiction debut *Talk Gertie to Me*. Shortly after the sale of that book, she was invited to join the agency that represented her, beginning first by combing the slush piles for talent and eventually working her way up to a list of her own clients.

Lois currently writes the critically acclaimed Anastasia Pollack Crafting Mystery series featuring magazine crafts editor and reluctant amateur sleuth Anastasia Pollack. She's received starred reviews from both *Publishers Weekly* and *Booklist*. *Kirkus Reviews* dubbed Anastasia, "North Jersey's more mature answer to Stephanie Plum." Her numerous awards include having been a *ForeWord Reviews* Book of the Year finalist, a Readers Choice finalist from the Salt Lake City Library System, and the 2024 Killer Nashville Silver Falchion Award winner for Best Comedy.

Lois also writes romance, romantic suspense, chick lit, children's chapter books and nonfiction.

Connect with Lois at her website, www.loiswinston.com, where you can learn more about her and her books, sign up for her newsletter to receive an Anastasia Pollack Mini-Mystery, and find links to follow her on social media.

www.ingramcontent.com/pod-product-compliance
Lightning Source LLC
Chambersburg PA
CBHW022126280326
41933CB00007B/570